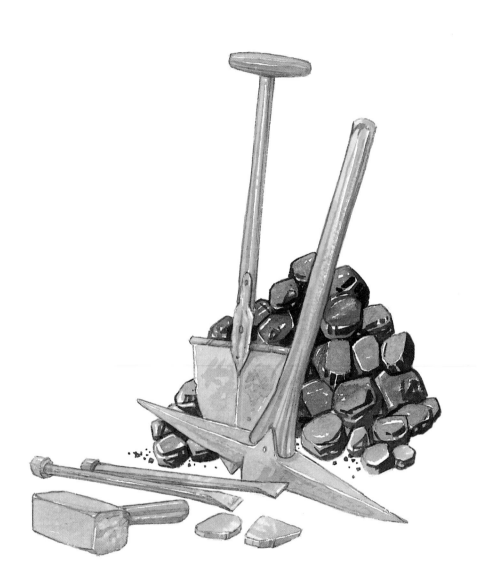

*Author:*
**John Malam** studied ancient history and archaeology at the University of Birmingham, after which he worked as an archaeologist at the Ironbridge Gorge Museum, Shropshire. He is now an author, specialising in information books for children. He lives in Cheshire with his wife and their two young children. If you would like to contact the author, send an e-mail to: johnmalam@aol.com

*Artist:*
**David Antram** was born in Brighton in 1958. He studied at Eastbourne College of Art and then worked in advertising for 15 years before becoming a full-time artist. He has illustrated many children's non-fiction books.

*Series creator:*
**David Salariya** was born in Dundee, Scotland. He has illustrated a wide range of books and has created and designed many new series for publishers both in the U.K. and overseas. In 1989 he established The Salariya Book Company. He lives in Brighton with his wife, the illustrator Shirley Willis, and their son Jonathan.

*Editors:* Stephanie Cole
Karen Barker Smith

Created, designed and produced by
**The Salariya Book Company Ltd**
Book House
25 Marlborough Place,
Brighton BN1 1UB

Please visit the Salariya Book Company at:
www.salariya.com

Published in Great Britain in 2002 by Hodder Wayland an imprint of Hodder Children's Books

A catalogue record for this book is available from the British Library.

ISBN 0 7502 3597 7

Printed and bound in Belgium

Hodder Children's Books
A division of Hodder Headline Limited
338 Euston Road, London NW1 3BH

# You Wouldn't Want to Be a Victorian Miner!

Written by
## John Malam

Illustrated by
## David Antram

Created and designed by
## David Salariya

an imprint of Hodder Children's Books

# Contents

# Introduction

I t is the year 1869, and Britain is now the world's first industrial nation. In the first half of the 1700s Britain was an agricultural country, and most people lived and worked in the countryside. Since then, things have changed. Factories were built in towns, and people moved off the land to work in them. Towns such as Manchester, Sheffield, Birmingham and Glasgow expanded and became cities, where noisy, dirty factories turned out all kinds of goods.

In 1851, the Great Exhibition was held in London. But this magnificent show wasn't just about the goods made by Britain's factories – it was about the machines that produced them, and the power that made the machines work. As visitors entered the exhibition building they passed a piece of coal – a huge, black block weighing 24 tonnes, dug from a mine at Staveley in Derbyshire. It reminded people that the great advances of the industrial age could not have happened without coal.

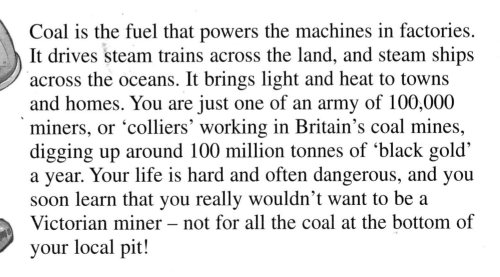

Coal is the fuel that powers the machines in factories. It drives steam trains across the land, and steam ships across the oceans. It brings light and heat to towns and homes. You are just one of an army of 100,000 miners, or 'colliers' working in Britain's coal mines, digging up around 100 million tonnes of 'black gold' a year. Your life is hard and often dangerous, and you soon learn that you really wouldn't want to be a Victorian miner – not for all the coal at the bottom of your local pit!

# Child slavery! The bad old days

## Children in the mines:

**TRAPPERS** opened and closed trap-doors to let coal wagons pass by on underground trackways.

You don't know how lucky you are! Until 1842, children under the age of 10 worked below ground in Britain's coal mines. It is now, in 1869, illegal to send youngsters down the pit.

**BEARERS** (usually older girls and women) carried heavy baskets of coal away from the coalface.

*Pit shaft*

*Miners waiting to go down shaft*

**PUTTERS** put lumps of coal into coal wagons by hand.

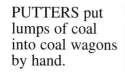

**DRAWERS** were children who pushed and pulled the loaded wagons.

*Pit props*

Some of the miners you work with began work as children or 'child slaves'. They tell you about the bad old days. There was no school for them. Instead, from the age of six they went out to work at the pit. For twelve hours a day, six days a week, children worked deep under ground in the dark, the cold and the damp.

## Handy hint

Hold tight! If there was no room in the basket, children had to hold on to the basket's rope or chain as it went up and down the shaft.

*Winding engine*

We're all slaves here.

# The pit! It's where you'll work

## You will be given:

### No. MEN DOWN PIT

A TALLY. Before you go down the shaft, you'll be given a metal disc called a tally. Mine owners know how many men are below ground by checking how many tallies have been taken from the tally board.

*Air holes*

*Wire gauze*

*Outer case*

*Lamp glass*

*Wick*

*Oil*

SAFETY LAMP. This lamp, or 'Davy', could save your life. It will warn you if there's a build-up of explosive fire-damp (methane gas).

The pits of the 1860s are different from the rough-and-ready mines of the olden days. Today's mines are thoroughly modern collieries, designed to extract as much coal from below ground as possible, sort it, and then send it on to wherever it's needed in the country. The pit never closes, and miners work in shifts. Some work in the daytime, others work at night. If you're on the day shift, you'll begin work at 6 o'clock in the morning.

*Screening shed*

*Cleaned and sorted coal*

*Coal train*

8

THE PIT HEAP is where mine waste is dumped. It's a mixture of slack (small coal) and dirt (pieces of stone and shale).

THE SCREENING SHED is where the coal is emptied when it has come up the shaft in wagons. It is then sorted.

THE ENGINE HOUSE contains the winding engine that raises and lowers miners, ponies and equipment up and down the shaft. It also lifts coal to the surface.

Handy hint

*Pit heap*

*Engine house*

You'll be lowered down the shaft in an open iron cage. Grab hold of one of its chains, or you might fall out!

*Workers' housing*

*Entrance to mine shaft*

Another long day ahead of us...

neigh!

*Wharf*

CANAL BARGES and steam trains carry cleaned and sorted coal from the mine.

# Down the shaft and underground!

## The descent:

DARK. You'll be in total darkness for the 30 seconds it takes the cage to reach the pit bottom.

WINDY. The cage falls around 27 metres every second, and you'll feel cold air rushing past you.

NOISY. There will be lots of noise from the clanking of the cage and the unwinding of the steel cable.

PAINFUL. Your eardrums will feel like they're going to burst, from the sudden change in air pressure.

More coal is needed every year. The trouble is, supplies near the surface are almost dug out, so this means colliers must dig deeper underground than ever before, in order to reach new seams of coal. At 500 metres deep, your mine is one of the deepest there is. As you enter the cage at the top of the shaft, try not to think about the long drop below you. Instead, make sure you've got your tally, your safety lamp and some food. Once the cage starts to fall, there's no going back!

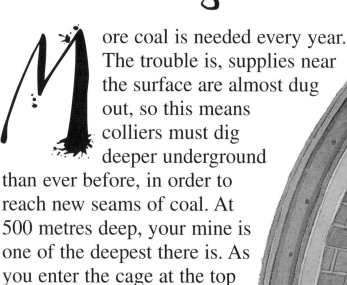

Coal tub

# Move along! Through the tunnels

**D**on't waste time at the pit bottom! Leave the cage quickly, before it is loaded for the journey back to the surface. You can forget about daylight and fresh air for the next eight hours. From the pit bottom you have to travel along a tunnel to the coalface. Miners on their way to the coalface say they're 'walking out'. It can be a long walk – up to 8 kilometres at some mines, especially those in the coalfield in north-east England, where the tunnels stretch out under the sea. It might take you up to an hour to reach the place where you'll be working.

## You will need:

GOOD BOOTS made from tough leather, with hard-wearing metal studs on the soles.

FOOD. Carry this in a little container, called a 'snap tin'.

A DAMP CLOTH to hold against your nose and mouth so that you don't breathe in too much coal dust.

GOOD HEARING so that you hear the sound of oncoming traffic. A pit pony hauling a loaded coal tub won't stop for you!

CANDLES, which are collected at the pit bottom. They're green to show they belong to the mine. Don't try and take one home or you'll lose your job.

MANRIDING. You're not supposed to do it, but you might get a ride in an empty coal tub as a pony hauls it to the coalface.

# Get to work! At the coalface

## Your clothes:

A HAT made of felt. You fix a candle to the brim and work by candlelight.

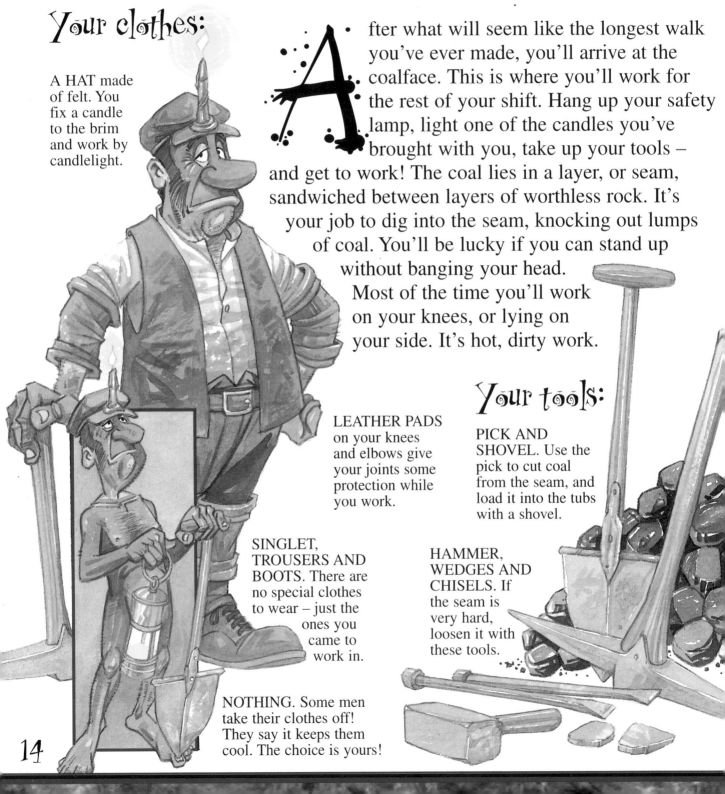

After what will seem like the longest walk you've ever made, you'll arrive at the coalface. This is where you'll work for the rest of your shift. Hang up your safety lamp, light one of the candles you've brought with you, take up your tools – and get to work! The coal lies in a layer, or seam, sandwiched between layers of worthless rock. It's your job to dig into the seam, knocking out lumps of coal. You'll be lucky if you can stand up without banging your head.

Most of the time you'll work on your knees, or lying on your side. It's hot, dirty work.

## Your tools:

LEATHER PADS on your knees and elbows give your joints some protection while you work.

PICK AND SHOVEL. Use the pick to cut coal from the seam, and load it into the tubs with a shovel.

SINGLET, TROUSERS AND BOOTS. There are no special clothes to wear – just the ones you came to work in.

HAMMER, WEDGES AND CHISELS. If the seam is very hard, loosen it with these tools.

NOTHING. Some men take their clothes off! They say it keeps them cool. The choice is yours!

14

That water's freezing!

GETTING CLEAN. When your shift is over, you'll need to wash the coal dust off you. Some pits have washrooms, but most miners get washed in a tin bath at home.

Handy hint

Count your candles. One burns in an hour so when eight have gone you know it's home time!

Hmmm

CLUNK!

CLANK!

# Take cover! Blasting time

## You might use:

**A DRILL CUTTER.** It takes two men to use this machine, which uses compressed air to drill holes into the coal seam.

*Stretcher column holds up the roof*

*Drill bit*

*Air cylinder*

It's a long, slow job, chipping away at the coal seam with hand tools. It's been this way for hundreds of years, but now there's a quicker way to get the coal from the coalface – by using coal-cutting machines. These modern inventions will make your job easier – all you've got to do is learn how to use them. They cut into the coal seam, making a line of holes or slots which are then packed with explosives, such as gelignite. When that's done, take cover! The shot-firer will set off the gelignite, blasting coal and rock from the coalface. All you do then is shovel it into the coal tubs.

Boo

**DISC CUTTER. A** large disc spins round on this machine, slicing deep into the coal seam. It's very noisy and makes clouds of choking dust.

**EXPLOSIVES.** Sticks of gelignite are stored in strong boxes which only the shot-firer is allowed to open. He's the explosives expert.

**WATER.** After a blast, water is sprinkled over the area to settle the dust from the explosion.

*Cutting wheel*

16

# Take care! How to stay alive

Luckily for you, coal mining is safer work than it was a few years ago. One of the main improvements came in 1862, when a law was passed which said all pits in Britain had to have a second shaft connected to the first. The owners of your colliery have obeyed the law, and a second shaft has been sunk. Get to know Shaft Number 2 – it could save your life. The new shaft is the pit's escape shaft. If an accident happens while you're below ground, and you can't use the main shaft, you'll use this one to return to the surface. It's also the pit's ventilation shaft, taking away foul air. Without it you might be breathing poisonous choke-damp (carbon dioxide).

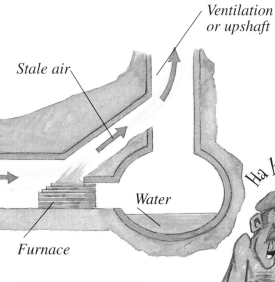

Ventilation or upshaft

Stale air

Water

Furnace

**AIR TO BREATHE.**
A furnace at the base of the ventilation shaft creates a vacuum. As it burns, it draws fresh air down the main shaft (the downshaft). Clean air circulates through the mine's tunnels and returns up the ventilation shaft (the upshaft) as stale air.

Time to buy a new hat again!

Ha ha ha!

18

## Handy hint

If your safety lamp goes out, re-light it at once. If you see the gauze around it glowing, and the flame getting brighter, that's telling you there's an explosive gas in the air and it's time to leave!

## The rules:

NO SMOKING. If you're caught smoking or with matches underground, you'll be fined. You could lose your job.

USE THE PROPS. Be sure to use enough strong timber pit props to support the roof. If you don't, it might collapse.

AGE LIMIT. Don't lie about your age in order to get work, or you'll be fined according to the law. Remember, boys under 10 can't go down mines any more.

19

# Help! Accidents do happen

## The dangers are:

FLOODS happen when miners break into old, flooded tunnels. Can you swim?

ROOF-FALLS are caused by explosions and weak pit props. They cause the most deaths and injuries.

EXPLOSIONS, caused by coal dust and the dreaded fire-damp, could blow you and the mine to bits!

DEADLY GAS, such as poisonous choke-damp, is mostly carbon dioxide, an invisible killer.

Even though you're working at a modern pit, where every collier carries his own personal 'Davy', and some take canaries with them to sniff out choke-damp, accidents still happen. Some you'll get used to, such as minor cuts and bruises which happen every day, but others are far more dangerous. Pockets of gas can easily build up, and if you come across one you'll either be blasted to smithereens or left gasping for air. It's no wonder that most miners don't live much beyond their 49th birthday – about ten years less than the average age for men in Britain in the 1860s. Mining is bad for your health. Even after you leave the industry there are coal-mining diseases which might be with you for the rest of your life.

## You might suffer from:

AMPUTATIONS. Falling rocks and accidents with tools and machines might do this to you.

BLACK LUNG. Coal dust in your lungs will leave you short of breath, and your spit will be black.

NYSTAGMUS. Years of working in poor light will make your eyes roll painfully around.

# Black gold! Preparing coal for sale

Although most of the time you'll be working below ground, you might find there are occasions when you'll work on the surface, such as when you're recovering from an injury. If that happens to you, you'll probably be put to work in the screening shed. It's a large building where the coal is sorted and made ready for sale. Most of the workers in here are women, but there are also men who are too old or too weak to go down the pit. The women, who in the Lancashire coalfield are known as 'pit brow lasses', move loaded coal tubs from the pithead to the screening shed. They tip the coal from the heavy tubs and it falls on to a metal screen – a big sieve which sorts valuable 'black gold' from worthless waste. It's hard, dusty work.

## Women's work:

1 UNLOADING. Taking coal tubs from the cage when it comes to the surface and pushing them to the screening shed.

2 TIPPING. Emptying the tubs on to a chute at the screening shed. Each tub holds around 275 kg of coal and dirt. Some 1,000 tubs a day are tipped.

3 RUNNING IN. Pushing the empty tubs back to the pithead, ready to be sent back down the shaft to the miners below.

**4 SCREENING.** Agitating the coal as it falls down the screen, pushing slack and dirt through its metal bars.

*Metal screen*

**Handy hint**

Don't wander off! Restless workers are made to stand in a box to keep them in their place.

**5 SORTING.** Picking over the screened coal by hand as it moves on conveyor belts, removing lumps of stone.

*Thwack!*

**6 CHIPPING.** Taking large blocks of coal from the conveyor belt and breaking them into smaller pieces by hand.

**7 LOADING.** Working at the coal wharf, shovelling the cleaned and sorted coal into canal barges.

23

# Hard times! Trouble at the pit

For many years, Britain's miners have demanded better pay and working conditions from the mine owners. In the 1840s miners in the coalfields of Northumberland and Durham went on strike, refusing to work until their demands were met. Then, in 1858, the National Miners' Union was formed. It's a trade union which looks after the miners who belong to it. You'll find that most miners at your pit belong to the union. You and your fellow miners have decided to go on strike for better pay, and you hope that the union will help you. But be warned – the mine owners are a tough lot, and they'll try and find ways of keeping the pit working without you. Remember, if you're not working you won't be earning any money, so be prepared for hard times ahead.

# Strike action:

**PUBLIC MEETINGS** give you the chance to tell people why you are on strike. Try to get them on your side.

**NEWSPAPERS** will sometimes support the strike. If they won't, print your own leaflets and hand them out.

Handy hint

Don't forget the pit ponies! Bring them up to the surface, where they can enjoy fresh air, daylight and tasty grass. It's a sign you're prepared for a long strike.

**STRIKE FUND.** Ask people in the street to give money to the miners.

**BLACKLEGS.** Stop miners from other areas working at your pit.

# The mining community

No, business isn't good these days.

Your pit, like others in Britain, is at the centre of the local community. It provides you with work, free coal to burn on your home fire, and, most important of all, a weekly wage. In short, you cannot live without the pit, and neither can the rest of the community. Now that you are on strike, life will be hard. Since you're in the miners' trade union, you'll receive some strike pay, but it won't be as much as you were earning from your job, and it won't last long. And with little money in your pocket you won't be spending much in the local shops. A strike affects the whole of the mining community. One thing's for certain – you'll have a lot of spare time on your hands.

## Your family:

GAMES AND MUSIC. Play charades with your family, sing in the colliery choir or play an instrument in the miners' brass band.

READING. Catch up on stories you've been meaning to read, such as that new one about a girl called Alice who, like you, also goes under the ground.

CHURCH. Go to church (often called chapel) on Sundays. Methodism is popular in many mining communities.

Handy hint

There'll be no free coal while you're on strike, so send your children to pick slack off the pit heap.

What shall we do now, then?

# Your recreation:

PRIZE VEGETABLES. You might grow vegetables and enter them in competitions – long leeks and giant onions are favourites.

DOG RACING. You might keep a racing greyhound or a whippet. If you're a gambler you could win – or lose – a lot of money!

PIGEON FANCYING. You might build a pigeon loft in your back yard where you'll keep a flock of racing pigeons.

27

# Strike over! Back to work

The strike has lasted six long weeks, and now it's time to return to work. A lot has been happening while you and your fellow workers have been on strike. Miners in other parts of Britain were on strike at their pits, too. For a short time, it looked as though the country was going to run out of coal. The mine owners knew they had to listen to the miners' demands. Officials from your trade union had many meetings with the mine owners, who eventually agreed to give you a pay rise. From now on you'll be earning eight shillings (40p) a week, which is a good wage for a manual worker. So, put your boots on, check your safety lamp, hold your head up high and get back to work. Britain needs its coal miners!

*Trade union banner*

MINERS' SONG
You colliers lift your hearts on high,
To God, who rules the earth and sky.
He only can defend your head,
While toiling for your daily bread.

# Reasons to return to work:

**NO HOUSE.** The mine owners have threatened to evict you from your house, which they own.

**NO MONEY.** The strike fund has run out of money, and you have none of your own.

Keep smiling! The mine owners might have forced you back to work, but they haven't broken your spirit. Sing a miners' song as you march back to work.

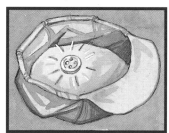

**NO FOOD.** Your family is going hungry and you need to earn money.

**NO WORK.** Mining is the only job you know, and you won't get other work.

# Glossary

**Amputation**  The removal of parts of the body due to injury or disease.

**Blackleg**  Someone who takes a person's job while that person is on strike.

**Choke-damp**  A poisonous gas made mostly of carbon dioxide.

**Coalface**  The part of the mine from which coal is dug.

**Coalfield**  The area over which a deposit of coal is known to exist.

**Collier**  Another name for a coal miner.

**Colliery**  Another name for a coal mine.

**'Davy'**  The popular name for the safety lamp invented by Sir Humphry Davy.

**Fire-damp**  An explosive gas made mostly of methane.

**Furnace**  A very hot fire, enclosed by brick walls.

**Gauze**  Thin wire mesh.

**Gelignite**  A powerful explosive used to blast coal.

**Great Exhibition**  A display of goods made in Britain and abroad, held in London in 1851.

**Manual worker**  A person who works with their hands, such as a miner.

**Methodism**  A Christian movement which began in 1739.

**Pit** Another name for a coal mine.

**Pit heap** A massive dump of stone, shale and slack.

**Pit pony** A pony used below ground to pull coal tubs.

**Pit prop** A strong timber support, used to hold up the roof of a mine tunnel.

**Pithead** The area on the surface immediately around the mine shaft.

**Safety lamp** A lamp which detected the presence of harmful gas in the air.

**Screening shed** The building inside which coal was sieved (screened) and sorted.

**Seam** A layer of coal.

**Shot-firer** The man who set off an explosion to loosen coal from the coalface.

**Singlet** A vest or undershirt.

**Slack** Small pieces of coal.

**Strike** When employees refuse to work until their demands for better pay or conditions are met.

**Trade union** An organisation which protects the rights of its members.

**Vacuum** A space from which the air is removed. This can cause fresh air to rush through and replace it, as in the way ventilation shafts work.

**Wharf** The place where coal was stored, ready to be taken away to be sold.

**Winding engine** The engine, usually powered by steam, which wound the cage up and down the mine shaft.

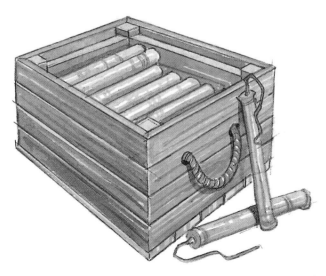

# Index